QUESTIONS FOR THE SEA

QUESTIONS FOR THE SEA

POEMS BY

STEPHEN SYMONS

UHLANGA

2016

Published in Cape Town, South Africa by uHlanga in 2016

uhlangapress.co.za

Distributed outside South Africa by African Books Collective

africanbookscollective.com

ISBN: 978-0-620-71155-5

Cover photograph by Stephen Symons

The body text of this book is set in Kennerley Old Style 9.5PT on 15PT

Grateful acknowledgement to the following magazines, books
and anthologies in which the following poems were first published:
"Spioenkop", in *uHlanga 1*; "Letter Home", in *Prufrock*; "Clifton 4th" and
"The Smell of the Sea (or Losing My Country)", in *Stanzas*; "Boyes Drive" and
"Muizenberg", in *Carapace*; "Death of a gecko" and "White Lies", in *New Contrast*;
"Mapwork", in *New Coin*; "Wordless (Townships, 1990)" (published as "Wordless
(South African townships, 1990)"), in *Africa Ablaze* (African Sun Press, 2013); "Death
of a husband by drowning" and "Emma" (published as "Birth of a Daughter"), in *Heart
of Africa* (African Sun Press, 2014); "Far below" and "Citrusdal", on *Aerodrome;*
"Behind curtains", on the *Kalahari Review*; "Second-hand bookstore" and "Knysna",
on *LitNet*; and "Call up, February 1990", part of the academic paper "Contemplating
shadows under a different sun", published by Stellenbosch University.

ACKNOWLEDGEMENTS

This collection includes a number of poems that grew out of my MA in Creative Writing at UCT during 2013 and 2014. I wish to thank my teachers and mentors, most notably Professor Kelwyn Sole of UCT. I would also like to express my deep gratitude for his inspirational guidance, encouragement and critique of many of the poems in this collection. Special thanks also go to my publisher and editor Nick Mulgrew for his respectful editorial contributions, design acuity and belief in my poetry.

I would also like to thank the following editors, who have included my poetry in their publications: Gary Cumminskey (*New Coin*), Gus Ferguson (*Carapace*), Etienne Van Heerden (*LitNet*), Michael King and Michele Beatty (*New Contrast*), Imraan Coovadia (UCT), Douglas Reid Skinner and Patricia Schonstein (*Stanzas*), Alexander Matthews (*Aerodrome*), Linda Kaoma (Badilisha Poetry X-Change), Duduzile Mabaso (*PoetryPotion*), Helen Sullivan (*Prufrock*), and Derek Workman (the *Kalahari Review*).

Special thanks must go to my close friends Tyrone Savage and John Steer for their longstanding support, encouragement and belief in the value of poetry. My friend, Professor David Keplinger of the American University (AU) in Washington D.C., also deserves thanks for encouraging me to submit my poetry to journals and competitions in the United States.

Many of these poems are part of ongoing conversations with my family and friends; my father and late mother, Peter and Nanette; my father- and mother-in-law, Peter and Rosemary; and my brother, Paul.

I am most indebted to my wife, Julie Etellin, and our children Thomas and Emma, for their boundless love, inspiration, support and understanding.

– S.S.

CONTENTS

Always for Jules

The waves bring back even things we haven't lost.

Yehuda Amichai, "The Seashore"

I

THE SMELL OF THE SEA (OR, LOSING MY COUNTRY)

A salted tongue of
        memory, licking cloud
                from the moon,

now naked
        and white as sun-fired
                bone. Its stillness wavers

through black trees,
        lifting drawn curtains
                and loosening sleep
into night –
        the ashes of dreams,
                too fine for remembering,

settle over a moonlit bay
        and shimmer
                into forgetting.

DEATH OF A SURFER

Death came in a whorl
of cobalt and white.

It sliced through colour and current:
        a scarred slab of cartilage,
        a slash of barbed wire,
        muscled grey sandpaper
against
        sea-softened skin,
        neoprened and tan-lined.

It took him for no reason
other than
        he too was at home.

Now shut tight
the beach is scoured —
        there's just the loitering of gulls,
        forsaken against
        the fractured bay.

Every atom muted,
        fathomless as the languages
        of the sea.

Kilometres up
birds of paradise
pen a secret calligraphy,
and in their imperceptible creep
a clarity is revealed:
that long after the last heartbeat,
a soul continues along its trajectory,
unseen,

      alone,

          and beyond this

               machine.

Mapwork

Your body is a map
spread out on a sunned table.
Hands try to iron out
its fold lines
like a sail snapping
          in the swinging wind;
          in an attempt to
          comprehend its way.

It breathes
of summits measured by fingers,
ringed by whorls of contours,
bunched into steep inclines
sliding towards veins
wending into what
could be lakes, dams
          even larger organs of blue,

defined by light into tropical climes
of luminous line.
And here I lie,
closer to fifty,
          still lost within its darkest territories.

Far below

I knew a man who slipped
off the edge of a mountain and slid
from the crisp view of
his camping chair into space.

In that manic fraction I imagined his life
uncoupling: from the disbelief
of a single misplaced step on iced snow,
and how within seconds

his flailing form had already
resigned itself to calm,
floating for an instant in
birdsong before the shadows
accelerated to gather him.

Onlookers came to view his slippage
over the flashed whiteness
before the heat softened
his terror to liquid. Some
ventured perilously close

to the precipice, hoping
to catch a glimpse of
his illegible form,
stretched over the
sharp black rocks.

Halfway there we find ourselves stranded, looking out towards a hazed kloof where folds of green crumple into shards of fynbos and stone – magnetic, like distant music on a windless night. But here we are, with a flat battery, sheltering under eucalyptus, in a town bolted down by midday. We wait. You reach for a book and I watch the inertia of life behind gossamer curtains. This is the heat's high tide. I swim from house to house, transfixed by the town's lunchtime motions, how shadows have detached themselves from objects and life, even meaning. A voyeur treading heat; a heat that disables language, so people simply eat their lunches of bread, jam and leftovers in servings of silence. Afterwards they seek out their mahogany bedrooms. More dust settles on napping tongues, on the thick lips of bedside glasses, brimming with water that tastes of heated copper. Time dozes too. It reeks of mothballs, rough, like the un-sanded panels at the back of their cupboards. Everywhere, blotched photos in black frames gather history. At the edge of the petrol station, where the forecourt crumbles to gravel, a newspaper brittles on a steel table as flecks of rust burn through white enamel. Curiosity lures me from my shadow island. My wife dozes with one leg just outside its safety; and even though I slip her leg back into shade, the damage is done. She will lotion a pink thigh tonight and smell of tropical fruit for days. All this place comprehends is a vertical sun and a deficiency of clouds. Every house burns at the stake and every surface has long forgotten the taste of dew. Somewhere an ancient telephone rings and two shadows make love before their afternoon shift; my wife stirs and a door opens. At last. Everybody needs somebody.

BEHIND CURTAINS

The remote traces of other bodies,
the ebb and flow of their privacies
ghosted against ripe orange windows,
until a curtain reveals a woman gazing out,
scanning the sodium dashes of street lamps
and the quiverings of long-dead stars.

Memory brims, spilling into the feline darkness –

> *a voice is calling over coastal distances,*
> *across decades of wind-smoothed shell,*
> *the saline residue of lost love*
> *tightening a skin of memory.*

She flicks her hair over her shoulders,
    I wipe the remembering from my skin,
and we return to incandescence
    as someone flushes a toilet.

II

Call up, February 1990

I remember a day when every father
became an Abraham; every son an Isaac.

But there was no poised blade breaking sunlight,
just the hum of idling buses,
treading the beginnings of day.

Somewhere rams were caught in the fynbos,
waiting to take the place of the Isaacs –
but no Angel intervened.

There, just the firm grip of sons' hands
and the impatience of engines.

On reading a war poem before sunrise

A good time to read or write:
when the house sleeps
and everything is stone and thinned breath.

A poem could begin here,
in the dream-lit waiting
of branches and birds.

Stillness hangs from the cold walls.
It frames the drone of a lone car –
or is that the breathing of the sea?

No –
it is the rush of the poem's blood,
its words fastened to
the quiet like beach sand,
in minute increments of roughness,
crystalline and salt-sticky.

You
brush the words away,
trace the rules of light seeping between the blinds,
let the first accolades of birdsong in,
and wonder how many storms
would scour a beach of sand

until it exposed its granite bones.

WORDLESS (TOWNSHIPS, 1990)

He collapsed
like a pile of books – wordless,
without a breath – muffling a clutter of
        steel,
        plastic,
        webbing and skin.

A puddle of black
grew from the dust and found the
muzzle of a rifle beneath his crumpled form.

He was gone,
shot through in the dark,
just twenty kays from my childhood.

A flare popped and tracer-
arced into corrugated black.

A woman wailed murder
in a language I had never bothered to learn.

Then, more beautiful tracer,
and the tinned silence of a dog barking;
the sweeping of our boots herding spent shells.

The radio hissed and crackled
    orders
    grids
    a SITREP for Tango Zulu whatever.

A swelling of quiet
followed like a bruise,
soothed by the guttural cluck of the Casspir.

And all of us – wordless,
    like the blanket that bulged at our feet.

SNIPER

Up there
his days rifled
to a burst window
with its teeth still
fixed to a shattered frame

And from his height
he would marvel
how man had managed
to dismantle the sun
with war

At night he aimed at a sky
stretched over a ribcage of trusses
and watched the stars tremor
as their light arrived
like rain

He died
floors up in that
shell-shocked room:
a space that freezes
the echoes of pigeons' feet

LETTER HOME

1   The shadows of the steel window frames
are drawn back
then released by a breeze
to reveal the sun-cracked gauze
that lets the flies
and mozzies in.

Pretorius sits in a slash of light
brushing the opvok out of his boots
whistling
– more spit than sound –
as his hand blurs over the laces,
scuffing his palm
to the colour of his overalls.

We're all here –
some in shorts that have slipped their drawstrings,
others in vests with the life hung out of them –
cleaning rifles,
or licking lies into envelopes.

Beyond the base
churches are pealing for believers.
Drunken notes tumble into the bungalow,
swirling homesick motes,
drawing memory into sunlight,

so a happiness
that masquerades as dust
is held briefly by
the doorway.

II   *Ja, julle vokking naaiers*
       gaan nou lekker afkak
       is how it would begin.

       But before that:
       a shuffling line,
       dribbling fucks,
       forming in the
       after-lunch heat

       so we could drop sandbags
       into each other's packs.
       Slowly the weight would
       grow bones,
       gather flesh
       and sinew,
       and gnaw at our backs.

       Pretorius always stuffed a wet towel
       under his webbing
       to ease the rasp;
       clots of Vaseline, too,
       that would stain his browns –
       a bitch to wash out.

III   A week later they found him in the heads,
door ajar,
still sitting on the throne.
A skull flopped forward,
revealing a cracked bowl of bone,
a chrysanthemum of brain
dripping pools of blood, exploring
the flecked tiles and the butt of his R1.

It lay there
in the snuggery
between his toes:

the blackened brass casing
of his final letter home.

SHELL-SHOCK

A door sighs light,
then rides the wind
back in silence
several times,

As if someone
has placed a
cushion of air
over its mouth
to protect its fragility
from itself.

She opens
the kitchen window.
The door draws breath
then the sudden crack,
gun-shout loud,
and the frame spits glass.

In that moment
memory brakes hard
and the body reels forward,
inviting flesh to injury.

Spioenkop

Climbing the koppie
on a birdless dawn
with summer dragging behind us.

Hiking through the work of spiders
spilling dew beads and
skinning the same wet earth
where soldier's hobnails
crunched and slid
to reach a summit
christened with death.

Squinting away
from the sun-razed veld,
I look back down the climb
to where the last breaths of night
still shade the slope in slate and umber.

And in that moment
morning hews the incline
to a hedge of stone,
light splintered and
still twisted, deep into the flesh
of this country's history.

III

DEATH OF A HUSBAND BY DROWNING

She stands at the water's edge
feeling the sand
inching over her anklebones.
Her feet sink into its icy granularity
until something catches in her throat
like a small bird.

She shivers as a breeze
nips the sea-wet skin of her calves.
Or is it the thought of his hands,
white-knuckled and veined,
weighted by bags of shopping or
a sleeping child?

She stands at the water's edge
in the cast-iron light,
hours before the sun
burns away the smell of kelp air,
morning sheening
on mirrored rock.

Alone
(except for the distant blot of a dog-walker)
she watches the day ignite;
looking to the mouth of the bay.
Later, in those slowed hours
between breakfast and lunch,

as cupboards are emptied
and books are mothballed,
the smell of him seeks out her fingers.
And so she returns to the beach
across the stinging sand
to wash him away,

again and again.

GLASS

Sometimes he would let himself
wear the fragrance of her
on some insignificance of his body:
the back of his hand,
or the fold of his elbow.

He would lift those parts of himself
to his nose and let her memory
slip across the back of his mind,
like a blue window allows clouds
to skate over its surface.

White lies

I remember a wind slowed
by heat and burst stone;
how it snowed a skin of ashen flakes
in our honeymoon week;

How houses gasped
at the flayed mountains
drawing in the leftover smoke,
and the stillness that always
follows destruction;

How songs broke in bird's throats,
and language cracked in the carbon
gauze of bedrooms;

How even the whitest of lies
were flecked grey by the fired sleet
of their victims.

Second-hand bookstore, Cape Town

You'll find the poetry three rows up and at the end of the Classics section, can't miss it; past history, before cookery. He follows an aisle of shelves. Most are moulting – chipboard flakes. The quality of the carpentry annoys him. Filaments of paint run over the linoleum. They dribble down the aisle of the bestseller section – the quick reads snatched at duty-free or borrowed from a summer guesthouse; holiday sand still snug in the toes of a racy plot. Here, bookmarks are gravestones. He fingers out a laminated verse – a watercolour reminder of God's eternal love – complete with a dove winging its way towards a cumulus cathedral. Other books offer Happy Birthdays in cursive, ballpoint flowers, hearts and I-love-yous behind covers bandaged in Sellotape. *Darling Thomas, Our best wishes on your 10th birthday, love from Mommy & Daddy, 1971.* Handling the books leaves a roughness on his fingertips; not quite dust, more like a fine colourless sleet – the tidal residue of half-memories and forgetting. There are whole shelves letting go of childhood – spineless bedtime stories, illustrated books of knowledge and soccer annuals. A shamble of comics – sun-brittled, buckled, sticky-thumbed – in a shopping basket. Sunday afternoons of slow clocks and tea in lighted rooms. There are the books of the sick, the dying too, trawled from the reading trolleys of convalescent homes, the lamp tables of curtained seaview flats. Black and blue hard-backs that have shed their gold leaf. Emerald encyclopædias, infused with dreams of mahogany shelves in sun-trapped hallways. He wonders how whole worlds can be buckled into suitcases, taped into wine cartons. There is no poetry section, except a coverless *Paradise Lost.* It smells of burnt toast and carries the signature of a cup. The finger marks of its last reader have gathered on the edges of its cover. He holds the book for some time and looks outside towards the wet street. He shivers, frail as a bird's leg.

AN ARCHITECT CHEATS ON HIS WIFE

On a yellow afternoon,
in a hotel room
that opens towards the wind,
the circumference of his lie
weighing down his finger.

At night, as they sleep,
he rubs his chest at the point
where an ember of pain,
the size of a bead of blood,
will eventually take flame.

EVENING

A tired light.
A sky that has paled to salmon slivers.

Beyond steamed glass
there's the slight breeze-tonguing
of pine needles.

Larger branches sway,
almost imperceptibly, out of the
corner of a raptor's eye,
followed by the blunt barking of dogs
and a wash of traffic.

All of this carried towards
the far-off cawing of hadedas.

Over a stove
untruths are being told by a wife
of an afternoon spent
with a friend.

She turns from the pots
and coughs,

                    Just like the hawk
                    before it takes the dove.

WHEAT FIELD

We broke our journey.
I stood plucking
the barbed-wire fence
and let the view blur,
while you took to the stubbled field
with the light skirting your body —
sharpening a shoulder blade,
softening the milky beginnings of a thigh.

You stood there, transfixed by
the arrhythmia of a wind pump's blades,
watching it pump dust
into a cracked dam
covered with tufts
of sun-split grass,
edged by a sliver of wheat
the harvester couldn't reach.

Your camera aimed
at a blue crane.
Its lens flared:
    the bird, startled,
stepped into space.

IV

DEATH OF A GECKO

the night has turned to concrete
and the city is a   curtain
still   as the breathing of birds

a cat pads over moonlight
in search of prey
through the thinning heat
past pine needles
                    that float
                              on freshly-cut lawns

your hips are sketched
in tenuous veins of streetlight
that play   like jazz over the sheets
rhythms of shadow that rise
dip
then
                              slip into imagination

with sleep now cleaved
by the click   of an electric fence
                    I head into the night
                         naked
                              with broom in hand
to brush the gecko from the fence
and stop that metronome   of death

Summer evenings

The ease of this –
the horizon
heat and smog softened
thinning to a boundary of kindled pink

the parked clouds offloading
shadow over a far-off glint
a ship rolls and pitches in the buoyant glare
a foamed thread stitched
across a stillborn thought

Looking out, something wavers
eyes focus and then blur
to pending darkness
drawing in the blinding divisions
of a sun-fired inconstancy

Summer evenings are like the end of childhood
the nervous tick of sprinklers
the wet lawns that shimmer coastwards
offering emeralds to an indifferent sea

The future is immortal in this light
At my feet a column of ants hurry their dead home

INTO THE REAL POEMS I HAVE MADE

Again. Washing away what's left of day:
work, those actions of irrelevance,
their insignificances.

As if all that mattered was violence
and wondering how a God could never tire
at plucking away at existence, petal by petal.

Always the same slow shift of shadows
over curtains and walls
as the roof turns in its sleep,
and the enigmas of trees
screamed into the night.

Later, birds will relax their grip
and currents of cloud
will pour over the city
into the dreams of my children,
            into their sleep-gaping mouths –
                        into the real poems I have made.

EMMA

You ambushed your father
with an exquisite noise
much blood
a surgeon's smile
and a sudden ceremonious cut
frozen in pixels.

My daughter
you were completely ours
with your dimples
threads of hair
and fingernails of silk
still sightless
and exhausted by birth.

You latched to your mother's breast
found the heartbeat behind
her smile
and swam back to heaven.

And then, as all parents do –
or perhaps not do –
I thought of you a lifetime from now
made infant again.

SLEEPING SON

All ten of his years
>> firmly fastened to
the fetal curve of sleep.
>> The immaculate skin, perfectly firm,
yet scuffed and grazed
>> in all the expected places:
that stubbed toe of blooded black skin
>> twitched at by dreams
I have long forgotten.
>> The slightest frowning of his brow
as a fleck of light catches
>> his cheek.

>> How everything is centred on breath.

Even the tightening
>> of a sleep-clenched fist alters the frailty
of this moment,
>> of just standing here
transfixed by life's ability
>> to displace even the darkest spaces with love;
watching his breath
>> pushing and pulling at the
the taunt skin of his dreams,
>> and realising that is as close to peace
that I will ever come.

FATHERS ARE MOSTLY ABSENT

Inside, the air is more
liquid than gas, crimped
by the pool's heat and
laced with chlorine.

      ⟦ Relays of

                mothers and goggled children
                slip into echoes.
                Fathers are mostly absent. ⟧

Above,
there's the to-and-fro
dip and climb of a
starling tailing the swimmers.

Its calls careen over
the grey tiles.

MOTHER

A lone lush tree,
you gave shade
until autumn came
        indifferent,

plucking your leaves one by one,
a continual shedding.

Until winter,
when your speech faltered
to the cracking of bark
and branches fractured
at the slightest breath.

Finally –
the last of the birds took flight
in a fantail of white.

"It's better this way," they said
over sandwiches and tea,
as I watched the last of the leaves
swept by the coming of spring.

V

BOYES DRIVE

I rub away the splashes of salt
that have tightened the skin
on your shoulders

Your smile
looks out towards the bay
where a trimmed fingernail of moon
teeters on the fog

At last
a sea breeze releases the heat
from the throats of the sandstone boulders
behind us

Below
spades have stopped skidding over the gravel
and that fucking lawnmower is done
with the grass.

Muizenberg

I I miss
   your gunmetal skin
   dimpled and pecked
   at by a north wind –
   a shark-tooth patina
   multiplied over
   lines of surf stepped
   into sea haze

   watching mist-licked walkers and dogs
   their hunched forms carrying that grey light
   across wet sand
   towards anthracite
   breakfast and asthmatic kettles

   the copper surfers side-stepping
   ribbons of kelp at low tide
   and the citrus viscera of red bait
   sucked back
   into foam and grit

II   always –
the complaints of brakes against rail
that exhausted clack into the station
and a film strip of train windows
reflecting
the bay   snapping past
coves   terracotta roofs
reefs   and doric columns
waves   into

slow afternoons of dulled turquoise
heavy and
constantly   drawing life into shadow.

CAMPS BAY

Summiting the Nek
there's that buckled horse-shoe
of coast below
still cooled by an
absence of sun.

Driving past roofs
and curtained windows
weeping the breath of sleep
switch-backing down towards
the sea's voice.

So close you can hear
the drawing up of whispered lists
syllables brightening to brilliance –
then the school bell rings
and the children rush the gate.

CLIFTON 4TH

A splash of salt
catches an arm,
startling and sharp.

The body inhales its mortality
at the sea's matted edge,
of granite bursting through
kelp and surf-smoothed sand.

Everywhere skin is on holiday:
stretched over muscle, fat, ligament
and hearts beating against bone;

sunglassed bodies
becalmed on towels,
weighted by their cargoes.

A glistening flotilla
of umbrellas wait
for the wind to
fill their sails.

TIETIESBAAI

This bay
searing

in calcium whiteness –
a midday rise of talcum

shell-white
beneath

bare feet desecrating
a wind-broken boneyard

of angels.

Knysna

I   All life hangs
between yellow and green.

At the umber edges of the afternoon,
a dog sleeps in its road-kill pose.

Scraps of cumulus
float seawards,
slate underbellies freighting the sun –
so close a forefinger and thumb
would snuff its furnace.

II   I've abandoned this poem
to watch my son's kite
weighted by a flower pot
inhale   and   exhale
        in a protest of
peach   and   magenta
        plumage

as birds with names
I still don't know
turn shrubbery to song;
into impermanence.

CITRUSDAL

A large sky
moves over the valley.
It carries something
beyond itself,
slowly and with great reverence
into the distances of haze.

A meerkat slips into shadow
gleaming with stealth and sudden cool.
Below, budding orchards snag the
chords of dovesong, until only the wind remains.

Midday breathes over the house.
The roof arches its tin back
and scatters the starlings in an arc of fright.

Later, my wife will return from her walk
over rust gravel, where every broken
stone is a crumb of an infinitely deeper time,
and a buzzard will wheel above our embrace,
homeless, like a banished god.

QUESTIONS FOR THE SEA

16h30

The beach is stunned
by a day's worth of heat –
a blue and squinted view
crammed with umbrellas,
towels and glazed bodies;
framed by the peals of children,
broken by the collapse
of shorebreak.

Out in the bay
kelp gulls bank skywards
with gale-frayed feathers;
they elbow higher,
tuck their wings,
then dive into a school of mullet
caught in the rip.

I am standing in the shallows –
calf-deep,
wetsuited –
watching the gulls gorge themselves
as the last minutes of heat
liquefy to veins of sweat
between neoprene and skin.

Soon, towels will be cracking in the wind
and families will slog back
to suffocated cars,
leaving vacant plots
of flesh-smoothed sand.

Beyond the surf
an inflatable dolphin is skipping
past the gulls –

a plastic punctuation

chasing an unanswerable question.

18H20

Is this where
the ocean trawls
sound from the land,
gifts it to the gulls,
then pours the
leftovers from shells
into our ears?

19h00

This is a place
conceived by bone

Thick with wind
gnawing at a shoreline
strewn with tidal slicks of feathers
and foamed strandings –
mostly dead, picked at.

20н35

Footprints
from the high-water mark.
Life is wrought into
sun-brittled flats
of shell and seaweed, dust
that fills follicles and mats hair
into new arguments.

Above,
the gulls wail solitude
slipping into blinding light
re-appearing to skim
the white capped swells

There,
over the swaying mops of kelp
and glinted thighs of rocks
incessant motion is pressed
into incessant sound.

21H45

Somewhere a fisherman is praying
his way through a storm.

Yet, what part of your body
has turned to pewter
in this hook of ocean,
as the moon lulls you
and the city lights ride
your tides?

23н10

Do you feel the ceaseless rubbing
of bone and timber
that lies wrecked
beneath your skin,

held under by a black tonnage
beyond maps
and human claim?

05H45

What of those days
before this city,
millions of mornings ago,
when the bellies of whales
would have skimmed these roofs?

And what of the shadows of
great cartilaginous fish
patrolling these streets
of barking dogs
and swimming pools?

07H30

Why have we mapped
your body into seas,
bays and oceans —

Named your limbs
where there are only
blue-green
voyagings of current?

08H50

Are the shells
that we hold to our ears
still part of you?

Is what we hear
the rushing of your blood
and not ours?

10H05

Where do you plot your violence,
summon gales and
seduce chop into swell?

Who ushers your breath under doors,
through gaps and vents
until it bubbles to rust,

and salts away
windows with
perfect views?

MIDDAY

Looking out
towards a nebula of heat
stretched across the horizon,

I wonder
how these slopes
can carry the weight
of so many houses.

How are these words
more or less
than prayer?

ALSO FROM

Failing Maths and My Other Crimes by Thabo Jijana
WINNER OF THE 2016 INGRID JONKER PRIZE FOR POETRY

Matric Rage by Genna Gardini
COMMENDED FOR THE 2016 INGRID JONKER PRIZE FOR POETRY

the myth of this is that we're all in this together by Nick Mulgrew

AVAILABLE FROM GOOD BOOKSTORES IN SOUTH AFRICA
& FROM THE AFRICAN BOOKS COLLECTIVE ELSEWHERE
IN PRINT AND DIGITAL

UHLANGAPRESS.CO.ZA

Printed in the United States
By Bookmasters